WORK IN THE
PROFESSIONAL SPORTS INDUSTRY

by Greg Kerstetter

BrightP◆int Press

San Diego, CA

BrightPoint Press

© 2020 BrightPoint Press
an imprint of ReferencePoint Press, Inc.
Printed in the United States

For more information, contact:
BrightPoint Press
PO Box 27779
San Diego, CA 92198
www.BrightPointPress.com

LIBRARY OF CONGRESS CATALOGING-IN-PUBLICATION DATA

Names: Kerstetter, Greg, author.
Title: Work in the professional sports industry / Greg Kerstetter.
Description: San Diego, California : ReferencePoint Press, Inc., [2020] |
    Series: Career Finder | Audience: Grades: 9 to 12. | Includes index.
Identifiers: LCCN 2019005400 (print) | LCCN 2019010758 (ebook) | ISBN
    9781682827345 (ebook) | ISBN 9781682827338 (hardcover)
Subjects: LCSH: Professional sports--Vocational guidance--United
    States--Juvenile literature. | Sports personnel--Vocational
    guidance--United States--Juvenile literature.
Classification: LCC GV734.3 (ebook) | LCC GV734.3 .K47 2020 (print) | DDC
    796.023--dc23
LC record available at https://lccn.loc.gov/2019005400

CONTENTS

THE PROFESSIONAL SPORTS INDUSTRY

Professional Athletes

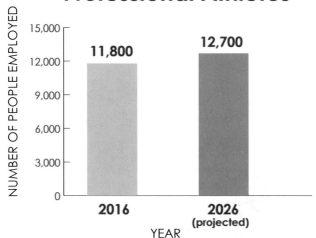

Coaches and Scouts

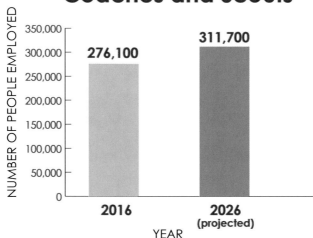

Americans' Favorite Sports to Watch (in 2017)

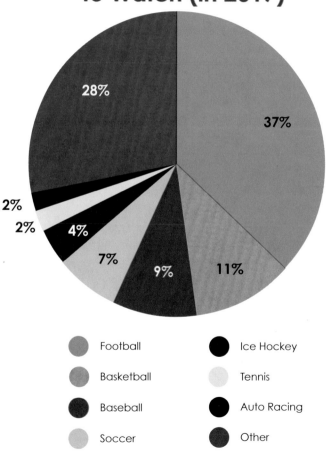

- 37% Football
- 28% Other
- 11% Basketball
- 9% Baseball
- 7% Soccer
- 4% Tennis
- 2% Ice Hockey
- 2% Auto Racing

Football
Basketball
Baseball
Soccer

Ice Hockey
Tennis
Auto Racing
Other

WHAT IS THE PROFESSIONAL SPORTS INDUSTRY?

Fans crowd into a large arena. Lights shine on a basketball court. The athletes are in the spotlight. They are professional athletes. They compete for a living. Many fans are watching them. They are the center of attention. But athletes

Professional athletes compete in large arenas or stadiums. The Staples Center arena in Los Angeles, California, can fit thousands of people.

are not the only people in the professional sports industry. Many people work behind the scenes. They help make the game possible.

Sports reporters share the important highlights of the game.

The players stretch on the floor before the game starts. Athletic trainers guide them through these stretches. Stretching gets the players' muscles warmed up. This helps them avoid injuries. Athletic trainers are the first ones on the scene if players get hurt.

They recognize and treat injuries. They know how to use first aid.

People sit at tables near the court. They type on laptop computers. They are reporters. They are paid to write about the game. They interview players before and after the game. They write articles for sports news websites. They help promote the sport and its players.

Cameras are mounted on the ceiling. They take pictures during a game. Statisticians review these images. They sit in a room with windows overlooking the court. The images help them study the action and gather data. They create statistics from this data. Statistics are numbers that give information. For example, one type of statistic is a player's speed. Teams use this information to improve their play.

The players warm up. They practice shooting baskets. They go to the sidelines just before the game starts. They surround a person in a suit. This person is their coach. Other coaches surround the team. They are assistant coaches. They make important decisions during the game. They decide which athletes will play in the game. They plan strategies.

Coaches motivate players before a game.

There are many opportunities in the professional sports industry. A variety of jobs are available. Many people around the world watch professional sports. Sports entertain and bring people together every day.

CHAPTER ONE

ATHLETE

Athletes are the reason professional sports exist. They play the games and compete in the matches. Fans fill sports arenas to watch athletes play. Fans also watch games on television. They comment on the action using social media.

WHAT THEY DO

Athletes compete against each other. But games are only one part of a

MINIMUM EDUCATION: **None**

PERSONAL QUALITIES: **Athletic, focused, dedicated, coordinated, able to work within a team, a good decision maker**

CERTIFICATION AND LICENSING: **State licenses are necessary for some athletes, such as auto racers and boxers.**

WORKING CONDITIONS: **Athletes train year-round. They often work more than forty hours each week during the regular season. This includes travel, nights, weekends, and holidays.**

SALARY: **The average pay for athletes in 2017 was $51,370 per year. The lowest 10% earned less than $19,220. The highest 10% earned more than $208,000.**

NUMBER OF JOBS: **11,800 in 2016**

FUTURE JOB OUTLOOK: **The number of jobs is expected to grow 7% from 2016 to 2026, or an additional 900 jobs.**

pro athlete's job. Athletes need to practice before games. They may train for hours at a time. Pro baseball player Erik Ostberg

Professional athletes play in many games each year.

spends at least ten hours at a ballpark on

the day of a game. Ostberg was **drafted**

by the Tampa Bay Rays. The Rays have

minor and major **league** teams. Both are

professional leagues. Ostberg began his

career in the minor leagues in 2017. Many athletes play in the minor leagues before getting to the major leagues. The minor leagues prepare them for the major leagues.

Ostberg gets to the ballpark at noon for a night game. Then the work begins. Ostberg first stretches. Then he practices his hitting technique. Next he attends meetings. He learns about the strategies his team plans to use. He also learns about the opposing team. At that point in the day, it is usually about 3:00 p.m. Then Ostberg works on his defensive skills as a catcher. He later joins the rest of the team for stretching and warm-up exercises. They practice team defense. He might also lift weights and take more batting practice.

Ostberg has dinner at 5:00 p.m. After dinner, he rests for a while before the game. The games usually start at 7:00 p.m. Ostberg and his teammates gather for a final warm-up before the game starts. Games last until about 10:00 p.m. Sometimes they go even later.

Sports have off-seasons and regular seasons. Off-seasons are periods when athletes are not competing. Regular seasons are periods when athletes

There are thirty Major League Baseball teams. Each team can have up to forty players.

are training and playing games against

other teams. Different sports have different

regular seasons. The Major League

Baseball (MLB) regular season begins in

late March or early April. MLB teams play

games nearly every day. They sometimes

Twelve teams make up the Women's National Basketball Association.

travel during the day and play at night. Players get a few days off each month during the regular season.

The schedule is also demanding for pro basketball and football players. The National Basketball Association (NBA) is a professional league for men. The NBA's regular season begins in October. The Women's National Basketball Association (WNBA) is a professional league for women. Its regular season begins in May. The National Football League's (NFL's) regular season begins in September. Pro sports games are played all around the country. Teams spend a lot of time on the road.

Games are not scheduled during a sport's off-season. All athletes train to prepare for the next regular season. They work with athletic trainers to stay fit. They lift weights and do drills to improve their performance.

BECOMING A PRO

It takes a long time to become a pro athlete. It requires a lot of hard work. Training begins for many athletes when they are young. Some pro tennis players started playing at about five or six years old. Golf legend Tiger Woods began playing golf when he was two years old. Not all athletes start playing a sport this early. But most concentrate on their sport at an early age. Becoming a professional takes time. Starting young is important.

A young athlete may join a team that travels beyond the athlete's city or state.

Serena Williams began playing tennis when she was three years old. She became a professional tennis player when she was just fourteen years old.

Traveling teams offer a higher level of competition. Children as young as eight years old may travel hours to attend matches or games. Travel is not always easy for families. It costs time and money.

Many athletes compete at the college level before going professional.

Children may also miss some school while traveling.

Many athletes play sports in high school. College coaches and recruiters look for top-performing high school athletes. They attend high school games. They also watch practices. They talk to athletes' coaches. They seek out athletes to play at the college level.

While many athletes go to college, getting a bachelor's degree is not necessary. Some athletes only stay in college for one or two years. Professional leagues draft college athletes. They sometimes draft young athletes who have not gone to college. Many of these athletes first train in professional developmental leagues. The pay is low in these leagues. But athletes get the training they need to become well-paid professionals.

LOOKING AHEAD

Many people dream of becoming professional athletes. But the jobs are few and the competition is fierce. Still, these challenges do not keep athletes from trying. The job can be rewarding. Pro athletes participate in a sport that they greatly enjoy. They work hard to achieve their goals.

FIND OUT MORE

The National Collegiate Athletic Association (NCAA)

website: www.ncaa.org/about

The NCAA organizes student athletics for colleges and universities. It runs tournaments. It makes rules that allow for fair competition.

The National Council of Youth Sports (NCYS)

website: www.ncys.org

The NCYS helps make youth sports safe. It also helps improve coaching techniques. It finds new and talented young athletes.

The National Federation of State High School Associations (NFHS)

website: www.nfhs.org/who-we-are/aboutus

The NFHS establishes standards for high school sports competitions. It holds meetings. Sports officials receive training at these meetings.

CHAPTER TWO

ATHLETIC TRAINER

A thletic trainers have an important role in the professional sports industry. Some work for teams. Others work for individual athletes. Athletes push their bodies hard to perform at a high level. That effort can lead to injuries. Trainers help athletes get back to top form after an injury. They also work with athletes to keep

MINIMUM EDUCATION: Bachelor's or master's
degree in athletic training

PERSONAL QUALITIES: Compassionate, hard
working, a good communicator, detail-oriented,
calm under pressure

CERTIFICATION AND LICENSING: A license from
the Board of Certification for the Athletic Trainer is
required in most states.

WORKING CONDITIONS: Many athletic trainers
work odd hours. They also travel with teams.

SALARY: The average pay for athletic trainers in
2017 was $46,630 per year. The lowest 10%
earned less than $30,740. The highest 10%
earned more than $69,530.

NUMBER OF JOBS: 27,800 in 2016

FUTURE JOB OUTLOOK: The number of jobs is
expected to grow 23% from 2016 to 2026, or an
additional 6,300 jobs.

them healthy. They teach athletes how to

remain flexible and strong. Some trainers

help athletes improve their skills.

Athletic trainers help athletes stretch to avoid injuries.

WHAT THEY DO

Trainers start their days before a game or

competition. They work in a training room.

Athletes come to the room to get treated for injuries. Trainers use athletic tape to support sprained ankles. Tape also supports weak joints such as wrists. Athletes who have minor injuries may want to continue competing. Trainers help them do this. Trainers suggest the right brace to wear. They apply pads to protect injuries.

Trainers watch athletes during practices and games. Players may be prone to certain types of injuries depending on the sport. Ankle sprains are common among basketball players. Football players are prone to many types of injuries. Football is an aggressive sport. Players run into each other.

Trainers prepare for common and uncommon injuries. They know first aid. They also consider weather conditions if athletes are competing outside. Cold weather can cause frostbite. Heat can cause dehydration. It can also cause heat stroke. Trainers keep an eye out for these conditions. They make sure athletes drink plenty of water.

A trainer's main goal is to prevent injuries. But no matter what a trainer does, athletes sometimes get injured. The trainer is often

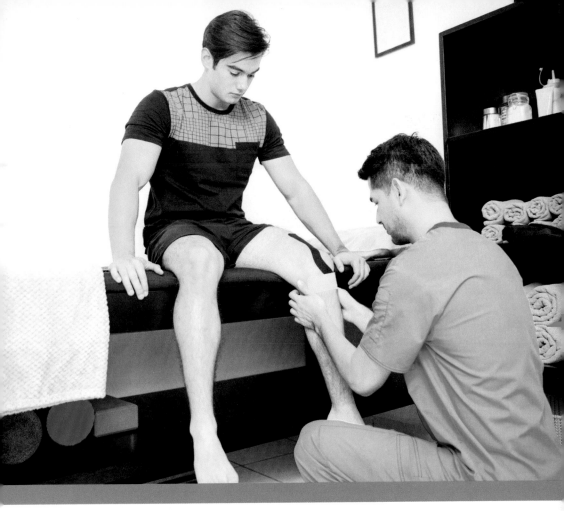

Athletic tape is often used to support joints. This can help reduce pain from injuries.

the first person to treat an injury. The trainer

first **diagnoses** the injury. A diagnosis helps

the trainer know how to treat the injury.

Trainers work with doctors. They help make

Athletic trainers are often the first people to assess an injured player.

treatment plans. Trainers follow these plans to treat the athletes.

Trainers treat athletes after a game. They provide ice for minor strains. Ice slows down swelling. Trainers suggest stretches to help with muscle pulls.

Trainers help athletes remain healthy. They give athletes plans for how to take care of their bodies. Those plans include strengthening exercises and stretches.

TRAINING

Athletic trainers must know how the human body works. People who want to become trainers need a science background. They can take science classes in high school and college. They learn about different systems in the human body. This branch of science is called anatomy. Students should also take **nutrition** and **physics** classes.

Physics helps them learn about the forces that cause injuries.

Trainers need to have a bachelor's degree. Some colleges offer an athletic training major. But people who do not have this major can still become trainers. They can get a master's degree in athletic training. These are often two-year programs.

Most states require athletic trainers to have a license. This license comes from the Board of Certification for the Athletic Trainer. It shows that the trainer has

Athletic trainers may monitor athletes' vital signs, such as their blood pressure, during a game or match.

achieved an advanced level of education.

People must take and pass an exam. Then

they get a license. They become a certified

athletic trainer.

LOOKING AHEAD

Breakthroughs are changing sports medicine. Health care professionals are learning more about injuries such as **concussions**. Trainers must keep up with these advances.

Athletic trainers are in demand. The professional sports industry is growing. The need for trainers will grow as well. Athletes seek every advantage to succeed in their sport. Trainers help them stay on the field or court.

FIND OUT MORE

The Board of Certification for the Athletic Trainer (BOC)

website: www.bocatc.org/about-us#what-is-an-athletic-trainer

The BOC creates the standards for becoming an athletic trainer. It helps people become certified athletic trainers.

The National Athletic Trainers' Association (NATA)

website: www.nata.org/about

NATA supports athletic trainers. More than 45,000 trainers belong to the group. Its mission is to promote athletic training.

CHAPTER THREE

COACH

Coaches lead sports teams. Some work for professional sports teams. Others work for amateur teams. High school and college athletes are on amateur teams. They participate in sports as a pastime, not as a job.

Coaches have many roles. They are teachers, motivators, and planners. They spend a lot of time with their teams. They

MINIMUM EDUCATION: Bachelor's degree or experience playing a sport

PERSONAL QUALITIES: Dedicated, resourceful, a good leader, a skilled communicator, a good decision maker

CERTIFICATION AND LICENSING: Some states require coaches to have a license. Coaches may also need **CPR** and first aid training.

WORKING CONDITIONS: Coaches travel and work long hours during the regular season.

SALARY: The average pay for coaches and scouts in 2017 was $32,270 per year. The lowest 10% earned less than $18,670. The highest 10% earned more than $75,400.

NUMBER OF JOBS: 276,100 in 2016 (not all at the professional level)

FUTURE JOB OUTLOOK: The number of jobs is expected to grow 13% from 2016 to 2026, or an additional 35,700 jobs.

get to know each athlete. They know how

each player can contribute to the team.

They motivate players to work together.

Coaches make sure all players understand the team's strategy.

WHAT THEY DO

Coaches help sports teams become

successful. They have a plan from the

start of a season to the end. They arrange

practice sessions. They develop strategies. Their guidance helps teams win.

Some coaches only work with individual athletes. For example, tennis and golf are not team sports. Coaches may work with tennis players or golfers. They help athletes train and improve their skills. Craig Kardon coaches professional tennis players. He has been a coach for about thirty years. He said, "I love the idea that you can help somebody even if they have an accomplished game and make them a little bit better."

Coaches help choose athletes to be part of a team. They work with scouts to find new athletes. They consider how the athlete would fit into their team. They look for athletes who have certain skills or talents. They often look for athletes who are quick and strong. They may also seek out athletes who have participated in semiprofessional or foreign leagues. These athletes have a lot of training and experience.

Then preseason practices begin. Preseason happens a few weeks before the regular season starts. Teams prepare for the regular season. Coaches teach players

Coach Toni Nadal (right) gives advice to professional tennis player Rafael Nadal (left).

the skills they need to win. They spend

hours each day analyzing the strengths and

weaknesses of the players.

Coaches are under scrutiny during the

regular season. Fans and the media often

Football coaches may communicate with each other through headsets during a game.

blame coaches for a team's losses. Poor

performance is sometimes the result of

poor coaching. The team's owner may fire

the coach if the team has many losses.

Coaches are under a lot of pressure.

Coaches work long hours during the regular season. They arrive at the field or court before the athletes. They watch videos of their opponents. They try to find weaknesses in other teams. They figure out plays and strategies to defeat other teams.

Coaches talk with reporters and team owners. They make sure their athletes are healthy and happy. The coach is often the first person to help when an athlete struggles.

During games, coaches call the plays that teams will use. The coach's strategies can affect which team wins. Coaches may

update their strategies during the game.
If one strategy is not working, they might
try another.

TRAINING

Many coaches are former athletes. Their
training for the job started as players. They
learned different strategies. Then most
became assistant coaches. Assistant
coaches learn how to lead teams. They help
the head coach communicate with players.
They work one-on-one with players. Head
coaches are often very busy. Assistant
coaches give individual attention to players
when the head coach cannot.

Coaches give press conferences after games. They talk to reporters about the team's performance.

Not all former athletes make good coaches. Coaches must have special skills. They must know how to listen and solve problems. They have to figure out how to improve players' performances.

Some professional sports coaches start out as coaches of high school or college teams. They work for years at schools, honing their craft. Coaches who succeed at the college level might be hired to coach a professional team. But it takes years of experience and winning seasons.

LOOKING AHEAD

Coaching jobs at the professional level are limited. The professional sports industry is growing. But the number of teams expands slowly. Coaching jobs grow as the number of teams increases. Jobs with high schools and colleges will grow faster.

FIND OUT MORE

The American Coaching Academy (ACA)
website:
https://americancoachingacademy.com

The ACA offers further education and resources for coaches.

The Positive Coaching Alliance (PCA)
website: www.positivecoach.org

The PCA offers resources for youth and high school sports coaches. Its resources include group workshops and online courses.

The United States Sports Academy (USSA)
website: www.ussa.edu

The USSA is an online university. It awards degrees in sports science. This type of degree is helpful for people who want to enter the pro sports industry.

CHAPTER FOUR

SPORTS REPORTER

Reporters work for television stations, radio stations, newspapers, or websites. They are also known as journalists. They tell fans of professional sports teams about games. They share news about players. Fewer people read newspapers and magazines than in the past. Jobs in those industries are declining.

MINIMUM EDUCATION: Bachelor's degree

PERSONAL QUALITIES: Persistent, hardworking, personable, skilled at communication and using technology, good at meeting deadlines

CERTIFICATION AND LICENSING: None

WORKING CONDITIONS: Many sports reporters work full-time. Covering sports requires traveling as well as working nights, weekends, and holidays.

SALARY: The average pay in 2017 was $37,690 per year. The lowest 10% earned less than $26,510. The highest 10% earned more than $195,520.

NUMBER OF JOBS: 50,400 in 2016 (not all in the professional sports industry)

FUTURE JOB OUTLOOK: The number of jobs is expected to decline by 9% from 2016 to 2026.

But fans still want news about professional sports. They are turning to websites and social media. Many reporters now post their stories online or on social media.

Some television networks have sports reporters. Michele Tafoya reports sports news for NBC.

WHAT THEY DO

Reporting the news about a professional sports team is known as covering a team. It puts reporters close to the athletes. They interview players and coaches. They keep up-to-date on team news.

Some reporters work for newspapers. They write stories for a paper and its website. They may take video and edit it for a website. They also post content on social media.

Other reporters work for television or radio stations. They interview players for the television or radio **broadcast**. They edit the video and audio. They do voiceovers of game action. They narrate what is happening in the game. Then they put stories together for different broadcasts. They also post content on social media for fans.

Reporters divide their attention during a game. They watch the game. They write their story for a newspaper or website. They also read social media sites to see what people are saying about the team. Matt Vautour is a reporter for MassLive. MassLive is a news and sports website based in Springfield, Massachusetts. Vautour said he often has three social media sites open at once during a game. Fans post comments about the game as they watch. Reporters join in on the conversation. "I'd like people to read [what I write]," Vautour said. "I don't care what format [it is in]."

NBC reporter Kelli Stavast interviews IndyCar driver Scott Dixon.

Each day is different for a reporter. Some reporters cover more than one team or sport. Others focus on one team or sport. Sports reporters travel frequently. They may follow one team to different cities.

Reporters gather for a press conference. At a press conference, reporters ask coaches and players questions.

Teams play many games. Their opponents change with each game. Players come and go, as do coaches. There is always something new to report. Eleanor Crooks is a sports reporter. She reports on professional tennis matches. She said the best part of the job is "getting paid to travel the world and watch some of the world's best sportspeople close up."

TRAINING

Writing is important for reporters. It is how they tell their stories. Television and radio reporters must write scripts. High school students should take writing classes. It helps to work for a school's newspaper.

Future reporters should earn their bachelor's degree. Some reporters major in journalism, but that is not necessary. Gaining experience is more important.

Many newspapers report on important sports events. They cover the sports that are most popular within a certain region or country.

"Every time you write, you get better," Vautour said. Many colleges have campus newspapers. Young reporters can join these newspapers. They cover college-level sports.

After college, many reporters work at small community newspapers. Community newspapers usually cover high school sports. This gives reporters experience and training. Reporters can later move on to larger newspapers or sports websites. There, they may cover professional sports.

LOOKING AHEAD

The newspaper industry is in decline. Some newspapers are going out of business. There will be fewer jobs for reporters who only write for newspapers. Competition is high. But reporters can find other types of opportunities. News and sports websites

Reporters and commentators help promote professional sports.

are growing. Reporters working for these

sites might also photograph games. They

might produce video and audio content too.

A reporter with many skills is more likely

to succeed.

FIND OUT MORE

The Association for Women in Sports Media (AWSM)

website: www.awsmonline.org

The AWSM works to increase the number of women working in professional sports media. It offers **internship** and scholarship programs. The AWSM also gives advice to women who want to become sports reporters.

The Dow Jones Newspaper Fund (DJNF)

website: https://dowjonesnewsfund.org

The DJNF promotes careers in journalism through **grant** programs. It also offers journalism internships for college students.

CHAPTER FIVE

STATISTICIAN

Statisticians work behind the scenes. They have important jobs. They collect and study data. They create statistics, or stats, from the data. The stats help them make predictions about teams and athletes.

WHAT THEY DO

Pro sports teams rely on advanced stats. These stats are called analytics. Special equipment gathers data. For example,

MINIMUM EDUCATION: Master's degree

PERSONAL QUALITIES: Patient, a critical thinker, a skilled mathematician, detail-oriented, good at meeting deadlines, organized

CERTIFICATION AND LICENSING: None

WORKING CONDITIONS: Statisticians work full-time. They may also work odd hours if they work with teams. Their hours may include nights and weekends, plus travel.

SALARY: The average pay for statisticians in 2017 was $84,060 per year. The lowest 10% earned less than $50,660. The highest 10% earned more than $133,720.

NUMBER OF JOBS: 43,300 in 2016

FUTURE JOB OUTLOOK: The number of jobs is expected to grow 33% from 2016 to 2026, or an additional 13,500 jobs.

some statisticians use a camera system.

The system is called SportVU. It is made

up of six cameras. The cameras hang from

a ceiling. They capture the action during

Sports statisticians use special computer equipment to gather data during a game.

a game. They take twenty-five pictures per

second. The cameras are connected to

computers. The images are delivered to

these computers. Statisticians study these

images. They track where the players are at

any given time. They can also track where

a ball is. Keeping track of this movement helps them create stats.

Statisticians study data to improve a team's performance. Different sports rely on different types of data. Baseball statisticians gather data about the speed of a pitch. They study the angle of a ball as it comes off the bat. Hockey statisticians gather data about the players' time on the ice. Statisticians study patterns. They use what they learn in two ways. They predict whether a player will continue to succeed. That helps a team decide whether to keep the player. Statisticians also give players advice about how to improve their performance.

The advice of the statistician is one voice among many. But a statistician's insight is important. It helps teams make decisions. Benjamin Baumer was a statistician with the New York Mets from 2004 to 2012. The Mets are a MLB team. Baumer said, "I was involved in all the major conversations about players."

Statisticians often work long days during the regular season. Baumer would get to work at 9:00 a.m. on game day. He would not leave the ballpark until 11:00 p.m.

PADRES		23 – GONZALEZ				1B	8:45

Scoreboard:

PADRES   23 – GONZALEZ   1B   8:45

10 ROBERTS   LF
24 GILES   RF
7 WALKER   2B
*23 GONZALEZ   1B
28 BARD   C
25 CAMERON   CF
34 BRANYAN   3B
27 BLUM   SS
21 WELLS   P

AVG .299   AB 529   H 158   HR 23   RBI 75
R 76   2B 35   SB 0   OBP .353
2ND-FLIED TO LEFT
4TH-SINGLED TO CENTER

BALL 0
STRIKE 2
OUT 1

	1	2	3	4	5	6	7	8	9		R	H	E	L
D'BACKS	0	1	2	0	0	0					3	10	1	7
PADRES	0	1	0	0	0						1	5	0	3

Padres   fns mk   sm noiz!

NOKIA Connecting People

Is the only player to record two multi-homer games at PETCO Park (7/14 vs. ATL, 7/17 vs. PHI)

23-ADRIAN GONZALEZ

Scoreboards display important statistics during a game in 2017.

Statisticians need to be available to the team's general manager. The general manager is the person who acquires or trades players. Statisticians give general managers information about the players.

Coaches can study statistics to see which strategies work best.

Pro sports teams have used stats for a long time. But the use of advanced stats is recent. Teams began using analytics in the early 2000s. At that time, only a few teams did this. Many people did not think analytics were necessary. They thought they could be successful without such stats. But soon, analytics were helping teams win. Other teams recognized the benefits of analytics. They hired more statisticians. Statisticians helped teams become successful.

Sports teams continue to rely on analytics today. Most pro baseball and basketball teams hire statisticians. Pro tennis players and soccer teams also hire statisticians. The Houston Astros won baseball's World Series in 2017. The Houston Rockets almost reached the NBA Finals in 2018. These teams have benefited from analytics. The Astros used analytics to teach pitchers to throw better. The Rockets learned how to score more points.

TRAINING

Training is needed to become a statistician. High schools offer math and statistics classes. People who want to become statisticians can take these classes.

Statisticians study mathematics. They learn how to set up computer systems. They learn how to use special computer programs. Most statisticians have at least a master's degree in a field related to mathematics. Some sports teams only hire statisticians who have a PhD. A PhD is an

The Houston Astros used statistics to improve their pitchers' performances in 2017.

advanced degree. It is a higher-level degree

than a master's degree. PhD programs

take about four to six years to complete.

Statisticians can get a PhD in mathematics or computer science.

LOOKING AHEAD

Statisticians are in demand. The influence of statistics has grown rapidly over the last ten years. By 2019, some MLB teams employed as many as fifteen statisticians.

It takes years of training and education to become a statistician. The competition for these jobs is strong. But the job can be very rewarding. Professional teams pay well. They often offer statisticians more than $100,000 per year.

FIND OUT MORE

The American Statistical Association (ASA)

website: www.amstat.org

The ASA is a community of statisticians. It holds meetings. It also publishes research papers. It educates people about how to use data.

The Society for American Baseball Research (SABR)

website: www.sabr.org/about

The SABR is a group of baseball fans, researchers, and writers. Its members meet to study baseball through statistics and analysis.

INTERVIEW WITH A PROFESSIONAL ATHLETE

Erik Ostberg is a professional baseball player. He was drafted by the Tampa Bay Rays in 2017.

WHY DID YOU BECOME A BASEBALL PLAYER?

I never had any other plans. I'm a western Massachusetts kid who dreamed about playing ball. I pulled out all the stops to do it. My social life is centered around baseball. . . . I work 9:00 a.m. to 4:00 p.m. every day in the off-season at the AP Academy [a training facility for baseball players in Palmer, Massachusetts].

WHAT IS THE BEST PART OF YOUR DAY?

It's the crowd that comes out to watch you play—that's the best part. I get to impact the next generation of players.

WHAT CHALLENGES DO YOU FACE?

The games go until 10:00 or 10:30 p.m. Then I get home sometime around midnight. It's brutal. It's long. We have two days off each month. I played 130 games last year. By late July [2018], my weight was dropping. . . . [But] our organization is good. We have mental skills coaches that help us. There's one in the minor leagues. He's the minor league coordinator. There's also a major league coordinator. I'm in a good place.

WHAT ADVICE DO YOU HAVE FOR KIDS WHO WANT TO PLAY PROFESSIONAL SPORTS?

Write out your goals. You have to be obsessed with your goals. You have to be goal-oriented and be with others who love it. You also have to have an approach that's open and be able to take coaching. . . . Then get in a network of people that loves what you're doing.

WHAT QUALITIES ARE IMPORTANT TO BECOMING A PROFESSIONAL ATHLETE?

Every kid is obsessed about something. Be obsessed. There's always time to do what you want. You've got to have a good work ethic. You also have to have an attention to detail that's off the charts. It's insane that I'm twenty-three years old, and I'm still learning how to hit.

OTHER JOBS IN THE SPORTS INDUSTRY

- Administrative Services Manager
- Computer Support Specialist
- Exercise Physiologist
- Financial Analyst
- Fitness Trainer
- Grounds Maintenance Worker
- Nutritionist
- Performance Trainer
- Photographer
- Physical Therapist
- Promotions and Marketing Manager
- Referee
- Scout
- Television or Radio Broadcaster
- Web Developer

Editor's Note: The US Department of Labor's Bureau of Labor Statistics provides information about hundreds of career options. The agency's Occupational Outlook Handbook describes the education and skill requirements, pay, and future outlook for each job. The Occupational Outlook Handbook can be found online at www.bls.gov/ooh.

GLOSSARY

broadcast
a live sports or news show on television or radio

concussion
an injury to the brain caused by a blow to the head

CPR
short for cardiopulmonary resuscitation, CPR is a process that involves pushing on a person's chest to pump blood through the body when the person's heart stops beating

diagnose
to identify an injury or illness from its symptoms

draft
to choose a player to be on a team

grant
funds given to someone for a specific purpose, often to help with research or education

internship
a period of training or work that helps someone learn about a certain job

league
a group of sports teams that play one another

nutrition
the food and nutrients people need to grow and stay healthy

physics
the study of matter and energy

INDEX

IMAGE CREDITS

ABOUT THE AUTHOR

Greg Kerstetter lives in a small city in western Massachusetts with his wife, Janet. He is a columnist. He also writes poetry. When he is not writing, you can find him on his bike, on a tennis court, or in his garden. He did not pursue a career in professional sports, yet he knows there are opportunities for people in that industry.